The Story Of Yorkshire

The author is a keen golfer with a Teddy Bear Mascot. She hopes that golfing parents will enjoy reading this little book to, or with, their children and encourage them to take up this great game. This is a true story.

This little book is dedicated to my Special Team; Deana, Emma, Jayne, Lynn, Rebecca, Ruth, Sara. Sarah, Steph.

Front cover photo by Linda Whitwam

Many thanks to my editors Mavis Green, Joyce Ironside and Roy Darcey.

Copyright Heather Cawdry 2017

The moral right of the author has been asserted.

No part of this publication may be reproduced without permission.

ISBN 9781540868312

With love from,
Heather and Ted xx

The plastic golf clubs are used by Tri-Golf. www.golf-foundation.org

Ted by Russ Berrie & Co.

Golf ball by Srixon

Golf clubs by Ping

ylcga.org

englandgolf.org

Twitter. Yorkshire Ted @Golfingteddy

First published by New Generation Publishing

Copyright Heather Cawdry 2014

All rights reserved

ONCE upon a time a toy maker made a lovely little teddy bear. He gave him a bright, shiny golf club and a special golfing cap.

Little Ted was looking forward to becoming a present for a boy or girl who would take him to play golf.

The toy maker put Ted in a parcel to send him to a toy shop but the labels got mixed up and little Ted arrived at a china shop.

He sat on the shelves with the cups and plates and he was very, very sad. Who would now take him to play golf?

One day a kind lady came into the shop and saw the little teddy with a tear trickling down his cheek.

'Whatever is the matter', she said.

So little Ted told her about the mix up with the labels and how sad he was to sit with the cups and plates every day when all he wanted was to go out and play golf.

'Never mind,' said this lady 'My name is Heather and I am Captain of a team of grown up girls who play golf for their County.

You can be our new lucky mascot and I will call you Yorkshire Ted.'

I will take you home with me and make you some trousers and a green jumper just like the team wear.'

Aunt Heather gave him a Yorkshire badge to wear on his new jumper.

Ted was so happy that he nearly cried again!

So the little teddy went to his new home where he met the other team mascots. There was a black cat with a large ribbon round his neck, Fred the brown cat and Simon the fluffy dog. They loved to play out in the garden.

A stuffed doll often came out to play but she thought they were all a bit silly and tried to boss them about.

Sometimes Little Ted was a bit naughty and tried to ride Fred like a pony. But the poor cat was very old and stiff and couldn't run very well, so Ted called 'Whoa there,' and jumped off.

Fred liked to have a sleep after lunch and then he was able to join in the fun again.

One morning after breakfast Aunt Heather took little Ted to her Golf Club to give him a golf lesson.

They walked to a nice flat piece of ground called the teeing ground. 'Watch carefully,' said Aunt Heather as she put a white golf ball on a little peg called a tee peg.

'Never stand near a golfer when they hit the ball in case they hit you.

You must stay still and not make a noise.'

She then took a big club called a driver and hit the ball.

Whoosh ...... it went down the fairway.

Aunt Heather explained that the fairway was the best place to be. The grass is cut nice and short.

Next to the fairway the grass is a little longer and it is more difficult to hit the ball. This grass is called 'The rough'.

Sometimes a ball goes into the very, very long grass a little distance from the fairway. This area is called 'Extreme rough.'

Players often lose their ball in this rough. 'Oh dear,' thought Ted, 'I hope you don't lose a ball today.'

Aunt Heather easily found her ball on the fairway and hit in onto the green. 'What a funny name' said Ted, 'because all the grass is green.'

Aunt Heather smiled and replied, 'The green is a special place and it has a flag in the middle. The flag sits in a little hole.

This hole is very, very important because it is the place where you want your ball to roll into'.

Ted asked if he could sit by the hole and watch the ball go in?

Aunt Heather said he could sit for a minute but then he would need to take the flag out of the hole. Aunt Heather said, 'I cannot hit the flagstick when I am putting on the green. It is not allowed.'

Ted said that he liked to watch golf on the T.V. He knew that golfers had to put the ball in the little hole. They got a prize if they did not have to hit it too many times.

As they walked over the course Ted said, 'I can see a big sandpit. Please can I play in it?'

Aunt Heather replied, 'Oh no, it is not for children and little bears to play in but a nasty tricky place to hit the ball from. You can sit on the rake and I will give you a ride.'

'Thank you', answered Ted. 'That sounds like fun'.

Aunt Heather explained that golfers have a special club called a sand wedge to help them hit the ball out of the sand.

Ted started to giggle. He thought it was funny to use a sandwich to hit a golf ball!

Ted was confused by the new words he had just learnt. Words like, bunker, fairway, tee peg, driver, iron, tee, putter, green, rough. Ted said, 'I think it must be very difficult to play golf.'

Aunt Heather said that she would ask David, the golf professional, to give him lessons. Adults and older children have lessons with metal clubs.

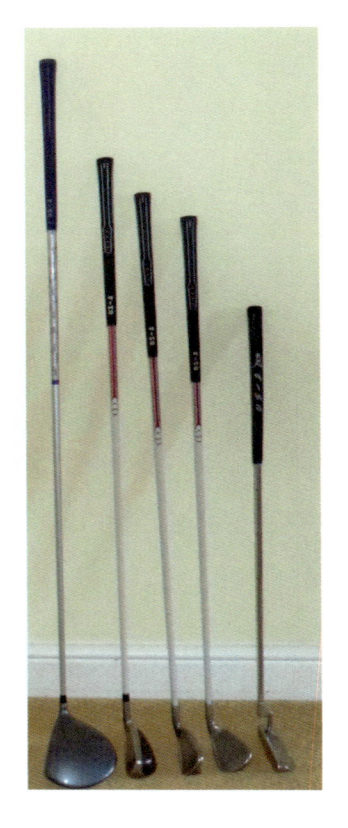

Golf clubs come in different shapes and sizes. Some are called 'Woods' but are not often made from wood. Woods have a big head. In the olden days they were made of wood.

Some are called 'Irons'.

Golfers have to choose which club they need to use. They can have 14 clubs in their golf bag but NO more.

Here are five clubs Ted. The big one is a Driver and is a wood. The next one is a small wood then a 7 iron, a wedge and a putter.

A putter has a flat face to putt the ball into the hole.

The game which some young children play is much simpler.

They use special plastic clubs and soft balls. They have a blue club to lift the ball in the air and a club with a red head which is a putter.

Little Ted sat by the clubs until the boys and girls came for their lessons. He was very happy to watch the children as they tried very hard to hit the ball properly. Ted told them that they had to practise every day.

One sunny day Aunt Heather came back from the shops with big boxes of biscuits, bundles of bananas, packets of sweets and lots of bottled water.

'Go upstairs', she said to Little Ted, 'And tell all the animals to brush their fur and pack their suitcases because we are going to the big golf match.'

Little Ted was so excited because now he was going to meet the Team.

Yorkshire Ted was a little shy when he met the Team but they all shook him by the hand and said, 'Pleased to meet you little chap, we are delighted to have you in our Team.' After that he felt quite at home.

Ted watched very carefully when the girls were practising.

Ted told them about his golf lesson. He said, 'I know that you have to stand on the tee and put the ball on a tee peg before hitting it. I know that you want to get the ball in the hole on the green as soon as possible'.

The team all said, 'Clever Ted that is just what we want to do.'

Ted said, 'Please stay on the fairway and keep out of the sandy bunkers and the rough. I want to be a good mascot and bring you lots of luck.'

Soon it was time for the matches to begin. Ted felt so proud to be one of the Team. They walked to the tee to start.

'Hurrah' shouted little Ted, Now it's my turn to bring you luck'.

Yorkshire Ted sat in Aunt Heather's backpack and watched everyone tee off. Each player stroked his little head for luck and he called out 'Good Luck.'

Ted walked round the course to watch the girls playing and he shouted, 'Good Shot' nearly all the time but sometimes he had to say, 'Hard Luck' when the ball hit a tree or rolled into a ditch or even went into a sandy bunker.

At lunch time Ted sat in the locker room with the other mascots. They talked about all the other matches they had watched in days gone by. They liked to read all the Good Luck cards which people had sent to the Team.

Ted made sure he told Fred about the golf he had watched that morning and gave him the results of the matches just played.

The Team had to play golf every day for five days. It was very hard.

Sometimes they splashed in the swimming pool to recover when the game had finished.

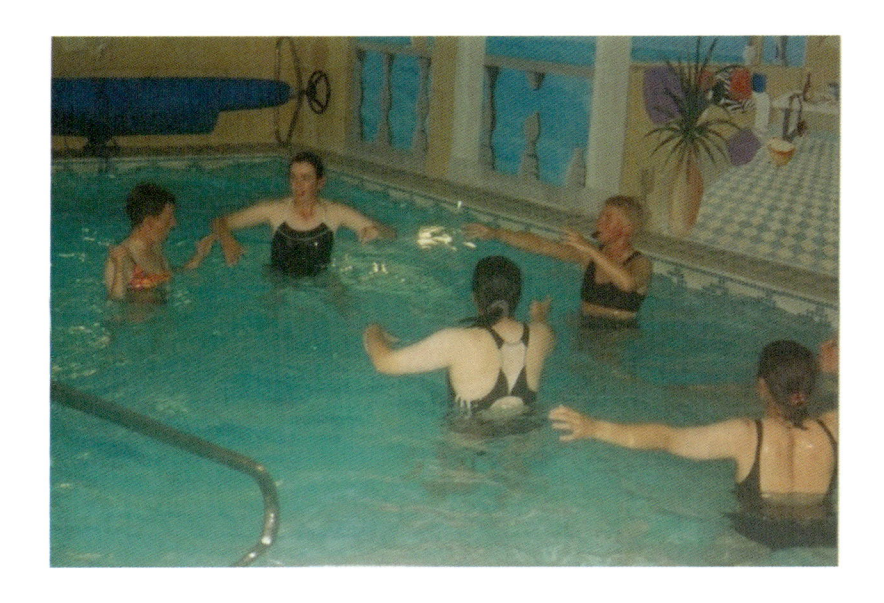

Some of the days were sunny for golf but some days were not!

One day it rained so hard that little rivers were running all over the course. The girls could not play their matches so the Team and the supporters went to the train station.

Soon the platform was full of large green umbrellas as they waited for a big steam engine to take them to a lake nearby. Everybody had a jolly day.

The next day the sun came out and all the matches were finished.

Yorkshire Ted was a very lucky mascot because the Team won all their matches to become Champions of the North.

The prize was a Silver Dog.

Ted was very happy to have another friend to play with.

Ted said, 'Please may I call you Silver and will you be my friend?'

The dog replied 'Woof, woof.'

Ted knew that Silver said, 'Yes'.

Everybody went home tired but very happy.

The happiest person was Ted the Champion Mascot.

He knew that he was the most important Little Ted in Yorkshire.

Printed in Great Britain
by Amazon